Wildest Poems

Macie Clarke

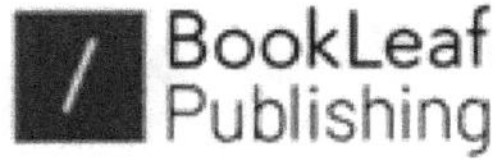

BookLeaf Publishing

Presentation by *BookLeaf Publishing*

Web: www.bookleafpub.com

E-mail: info@bookleafpub.com

ISBN: 9789357211475

First edition 2022

DEDICATION

To all animal lovers

If I was…

I am the darkest shade of purple,
The bottom of pansy petals that surround the
nectar.
I am the unpredictable sea. One minute I'm flat,
calm and gentle. Next minute I'm thrashing and
crashing with anger.
I would be a backflip underwater. Difficult and
complex, hard to stop when already started.
I am an R.V. Full of adventure, and filled to the
brim with crazy stuff!
If I am a shape, I'm abstract. My mind is hard to
trace and follow. Crazy.
If I am an animal, I'm a hyena: misunderstood,
treated too harshly but with a small group of
followers, and a taste for trouble.

Hyena

A cruel cackle pierces the night,
Here comes the trio of spotted frights,
Brownish-yellow with drooling jaws,
Large feet with fear-striking claws,
Eyes black and ears up,
Listening intently for prey in the bush.
A hump on their backs,
Brown mane and grey face,
Monkeys vanishing without a trace.
3 large canines,
Fangs now drip with blood,
Returning home,
As daytime comes,
To a pack of 9,
Led by a girl,
Enough food to eat and scavenge,
My favourite animals in the world.

Wolf

Howling at the moon at night,
Causing weaker animals fright,
A wolf emerges from his den,
Hunting for prey, his mates want ten,
Rabbits for the cubs,
Or a single cow,
Food is the thing on his mind right now.
His fur is grey,
His hackles raised,
Climbing into the ranch,
Sneaking past the bulls,
He finds a cow standing alone,
And swiftly takes her down.
Dragging it home,
He settles down,
He snuggles up to his mate.
The cubs all eat,
He goes to sleep,
Because at home,
He knows he is safe.

Eagle

Lizards scramble into rocks,
Rabbits hide, and away fly the flocks.
Into the burrow, flees even the fox,
Wildcats hide in bushes, though their fangs are
sharp,
As a shadow glides over,
And the canyon turns dark.
Ants hide in twigs,
Seen from 12 meters in the sky,
As hunting for prey,
An eagle flies.
Dead rodents line the nest,
On a mountain ledge.
Fluffy white chicks await the return,
Of their fearless mother,
As rats hide in the ferns.
Even coyotes bow down low,
To this godly-pretty bird,
Who squawks out loud,
Always heard.

Lion

A male lion basks under a tree,
Whilst females hunt for food, to feed,
The pride with cubs,
In the shadowy cave.
Sleeping at night,
Hunting in the day.
And when they're not,
They're on the rocks,
Snoring as they sleep.
Satisfied with some elephant,
And tasty zebra meat.

The males have manes,
The ladies do not.
They go and hunt,
They do not plot.
From herds and birds,
To zebra and ox.
From elephants and gorillas,
To the cunning fox,
Lions are stronger,
Brave and bolder.
Though hyenas are crazier,
Lions are lazier.

Cabin

On a hill,
Rocky path, fir trees,
A cabin towers over me.
Wooden doors with lion knockers,
And for your coat,
Sturdy lockers.
Wooden walls with velvet curtains,
Red roof and a brick chimney,
Light through leaves,
Shining dimly.
Windows viewing.

Treasury

Stone lions at the cavemouth,
Gold statue to the caves south,
A carpet of gold coins,
Oh, how divine!
A jewel and a camel,
Goblet and shrines!
Ancient books on golden shelves,
A sceptre belonging to the king of elves,
Silver stuff, enchanted rings!
Here you'll find everything!
A crown, a necklace and with the camel,
A majestic horse with a golden saddle.
Crystal implants on quartz pillars,
A mummy and a magic mirror.
An overflowing chest of gold,
A treasury it's mine!
Behold!

My cat

I have a cat
Unlike any other.
She likes to steal
All my meals!
Then she stole a brick from a builder,
A bone from a dog,
And a book from Matilda!
A football from Wembley,
Some instructions for assembling,
A chair from a cafe,
But what makes me happy
Is she takes them all to me.
I have a train set,
A nerf gun,
Anything,
Even a croc!
And a pair of stinky socks!
A guitar,
A sofa,
An ancient statue,
A drainpipe,
A backpack,
Tyrannosaurus poo,
Even a magical glowing mushroom!
Piled up in my bedroom!

2019-2020

2019, worst year I've ever seen,
In my long life!
Awful day and night!
A new small threat enveloped our earth!
A tiny lil germ,
An annoying worm!
Covid came!
Such a shame!
I think the illness god,
Had a grumpy day!
It began in China,
Spread like rumours!
Until covid took away our sense of humours!
Schools closed down,
We went into lockdown!
World war 3,
NHS against the virus,
Things were worse than they seemed,
We had to do our lessons on teams!
At home for all of year 3,
Something that really upset me.
In year 4, we came back.
For ages some kids just weren't there!
Fearful of corona, lurking everywhere!

As I write,
It comes to night.
Tomorrow is my 9th birthday,
My second one in lockdown.
It's lasted too long!
But when I am 10,
I hope things will be more zen.
As doctors care,
Send the virus flying into the air,
Life will be normal,
From Lincoln to Cornwall.

Planes

Planes can be green.
Planes can be white.
They could carry people far.
Or aid in a fight.
Planes can be dull.
Or planes can be bright.
Some planes look quite scary.
But others can be nice sights.
Planes can be low.
Or reach high heights.
Some fly at day.
Others fly at night.
Planes put out fires.
Save people stuck up high.
Planes are different.
Though they all do have wings.
One things for sure.
They're fascinating sights!

Happy Place

Nestled between two fir trees,
With a picnic set with ham and cheese,
Tulips make a circle,
With buttercups and daises,
On an island with clear water,
You can just be lazy.
Birds and squirrels,
Moles, bunnies and a horse,
There's also a friendly dog,
Living in the gorse.
The trees never blow,
For never is it cold,
The sun is not blinding,
Though still stunningly gold.
A sheep flock in a field,
With pretty little hairs,
Release wool into the morning air,
And down to your palm, they all descend.
The only downside?
It's all pretend.

Doom forest creature

Night falls, away you zoom!
Keep away from the forest of doom!
Have you seen the creature?
In the caves?
Coming out at night?
For blood it craves!
Larger than a bear!
With a pumas legs!
Back hooves of a stag!
Front of a tiger!
It's muscular bear body!
Tail of a croc!
Wolf head and snout!
Teeth that crush rocks!
It's blackened fur,
My friend it swims!
Encounters often end in 2 or 3 limbs!
How it climbs up trees!
In the dark of night!
When it comes over,
It is quite a sight!

Fox

Among the ferns,
The ivy, twists and turns,
Is a den in the roots,
Of a tree that grew and grew,
Mother fox lives there,
Her young cub too.
In the night,
Out they come,
So that they could play some games.
In the field, they played tag,
And a game of jumping,
Over some tracks.
And they paddled in a river,
The cold made them shiver.
A race to the reeds,
And the cub succeeds.
They play hide and seek,
Among these reeds,
Until mother sees,
Sunlight above the trees,
Dawns bright light.
The end of the night.
They run home to sleep,
Without a peep,
In their den in the roots,
Of the tree that grew and grew.

Dragon Summoner

15

Throw in the cauldron, a bulls golden horn,
Burn in the cauldron, a silver bush thorn.
Then throw in a brown bears brain,
And some fur from a lions mane.
The bones of a leaf,
Bark from any tree,
Teeth from an alligators snapping jaw.
Then, a wolf dogs amputated paw.
And finish it with 6 dinosaurs claws,
And a pet dragon will be yours.

Friends

I like my friends skinny,
I like my buddies fat!
I like them to be good!
Nah, I like 'em bad!
I'm a fan of girls!
Nah, I still prefer boys...
Little immature?
My friends do not play with toys!
My friends like ponies and kittens, yours?
We like fighting and monsters and football!
Small!
Tall!
Smart!
Dumb!
Frail!
Nah, I prefer strong.
How about you?
I like my friends as long as they like me,
Whether their weak or strong, I'll see...
Appearance doesn't matter when it comes to us,
But our heart, not our weight or gender,
And that's because,
I love everyone.

Dracocorn

Held in her horns, the orb of death,
Blasts down doors so you freeze in your bed.
Burns to touch, makes the strongest fall dead.
She wants to leave cities abandoned and fled.
Poison drips and flows from her wings,
She flies over streets to poison everything.
Burns does her fire, enemies she kills them.
Stalks to moorlands, preying on children.
The Dracocorn burns crops into husks,
And is the sworn rival of Dracosus.
Evil and cruel, give her obsidian, that is so
black,
To negotiate during any attack.
Her hooves are compressors,
That crush all heads,
The black hoof means certain death.
Venom seeping from boiling hot scales,
Frightens big to small,
From rats to whales.
Rots food and plants,
Wherever she goes,
She brings fear and woes.
Her dream she strives,
For eternal night.

A mix of good beast and evil,
She causes fright as she flights.

Dracosus

The moonblue light cast from two horns,
Guides dragons, humans and unicorns.
Away from danger and out of mines,
He helps you to stay alive.
His wings drop a substance known as cabeese,
A working cure for any disease.
His fire cures plague purifies water,
Protector of young sons and daughters.
On desert fields, he makes it rain.
Is he a hero? Is he a saint?
Calm and trustworthy, just offer an apple!
He'll rid you of woe, just with a tap of,
His silver hooves that leave a trail,
Of gold for the poor,
And bread for the quails.
His body and scales,
Drip good luck and pull the joy,
To women and man,
To girl and boy.
His magic brings food, as he flies musically,
To rich and poor, the whole community.
He protects the light and guards the gates,
Bringing in the worlds love,
And warding off hate.

Tigers

The tigress prowling in the deep dark,
Is large and muscular, the colour of a spark,
Her eyes are emeralds searching for a nice
snack,
She keeps away from the human shacks.
She's already got a hippo and two monkeys,
But she still has to feed her cubs,
As she does not want them to be hungry.
She has claws stained cruelly red,
From strikes to the neck,
To neutralise her screaming prey.
Facing off with angry panthers,
She is not going to die today.
Sleeping in her cave at night,
She huddles to stay warm.
Seeing creatures furious,
Shuffle around,
Their eyes silver disks,
Levitating from the ground.

Budgie

A fearsome predator in his own mind,
Circles the room, there's food to find.
Bites humans,
Who have no clue,
What this bird is trying to do.
Hangs upside down,
Just like a bat.
Sees human food, thinks,
'I'll take that!"